Lost in Translation
Adult Coloring Book

Funny and thoughtful phrases to make you think. One liners inspired by translating English in to various languages and back again.

Stress relief or doodle with animals, fairies, food and more.

©2021 Chris Johnson - All Rights Reserved.

Note From The Author: Reviews are gold to authors! If you've enjoyed this book, would you please consider rating and reviewing it?

GET READY TO COLOR

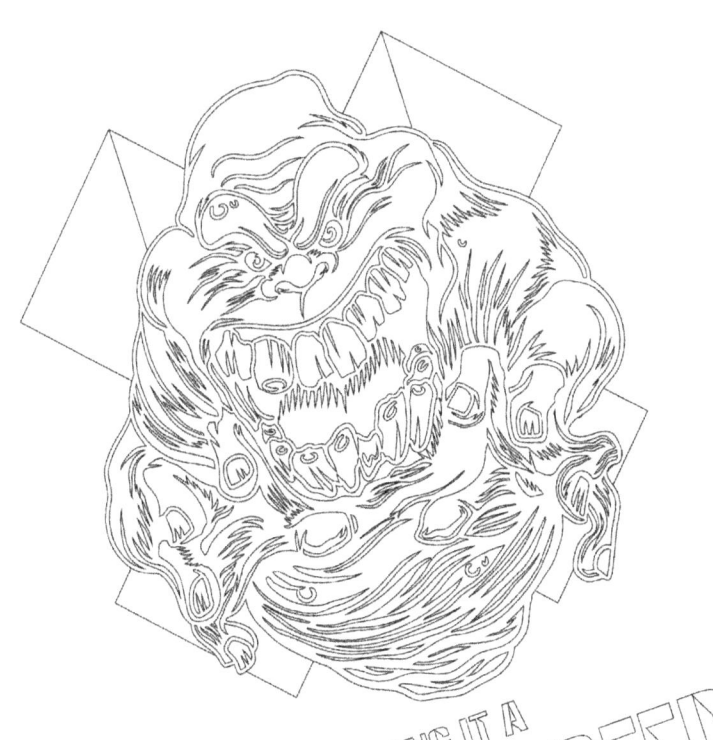

Varied Themes Of
One-Sided
Simple & Detailed
Coloring Pages

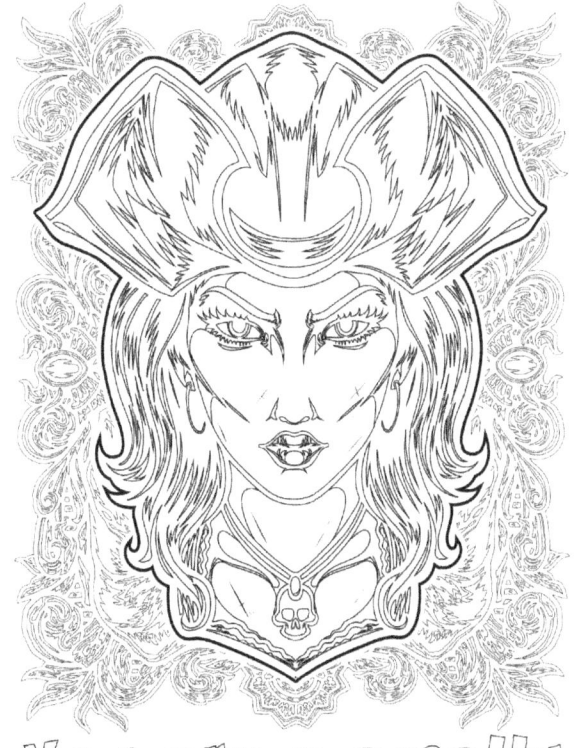

GET READY TO COLOR

COLOR SWATCHES

GET READY TO COLOR

Practice Page

GET READY TO COLOR

Practice Page

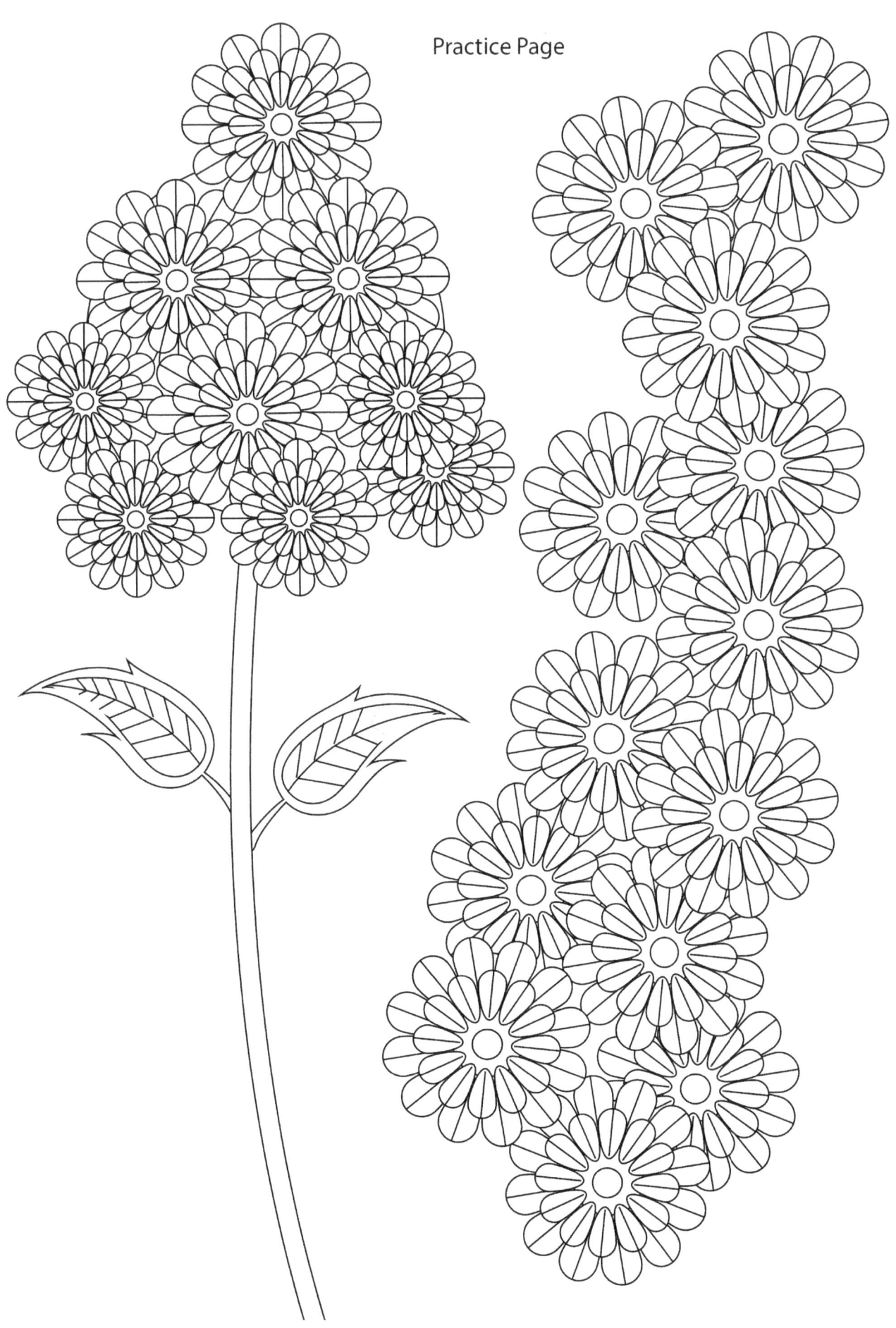

GET READY TO COLOR

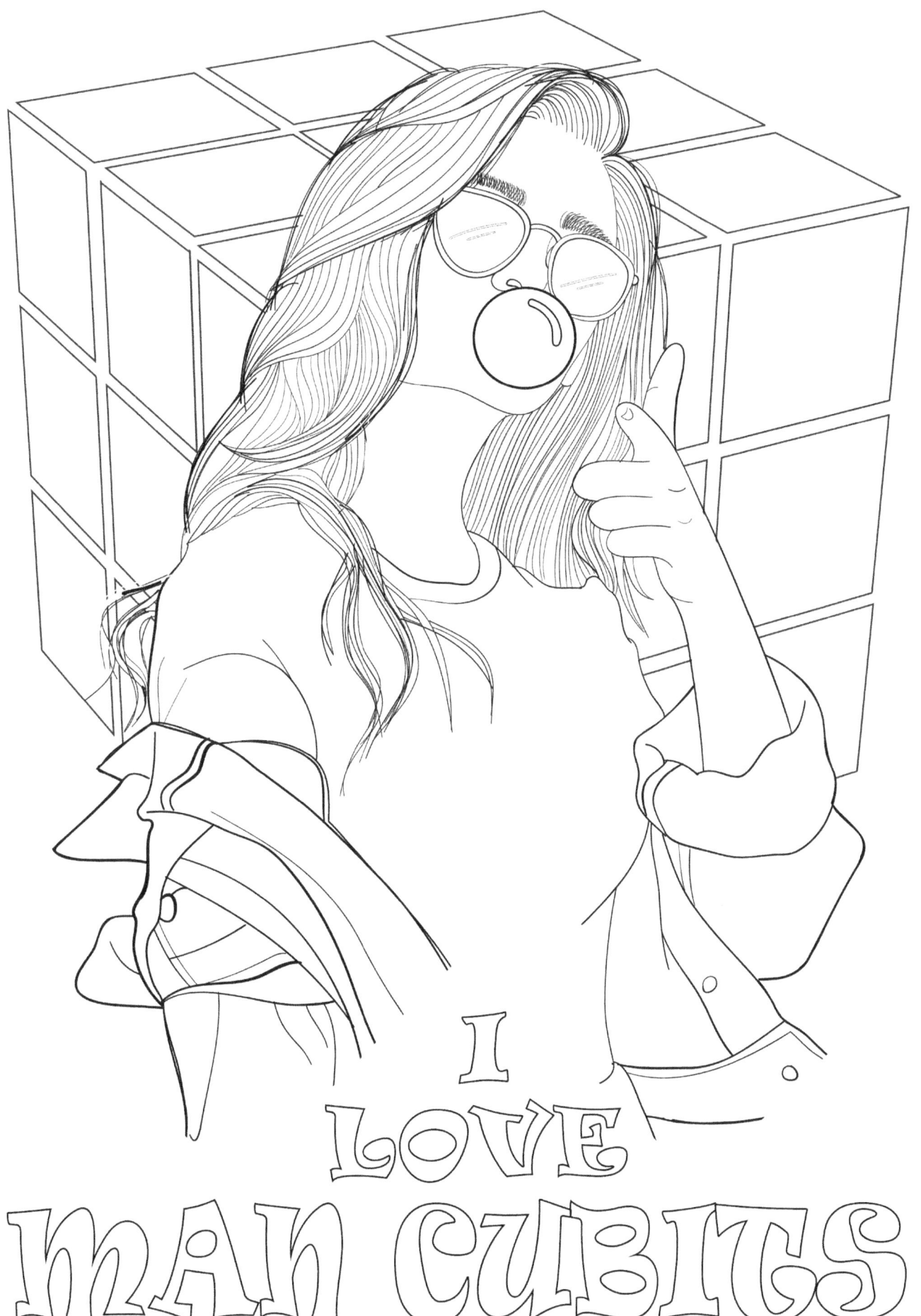

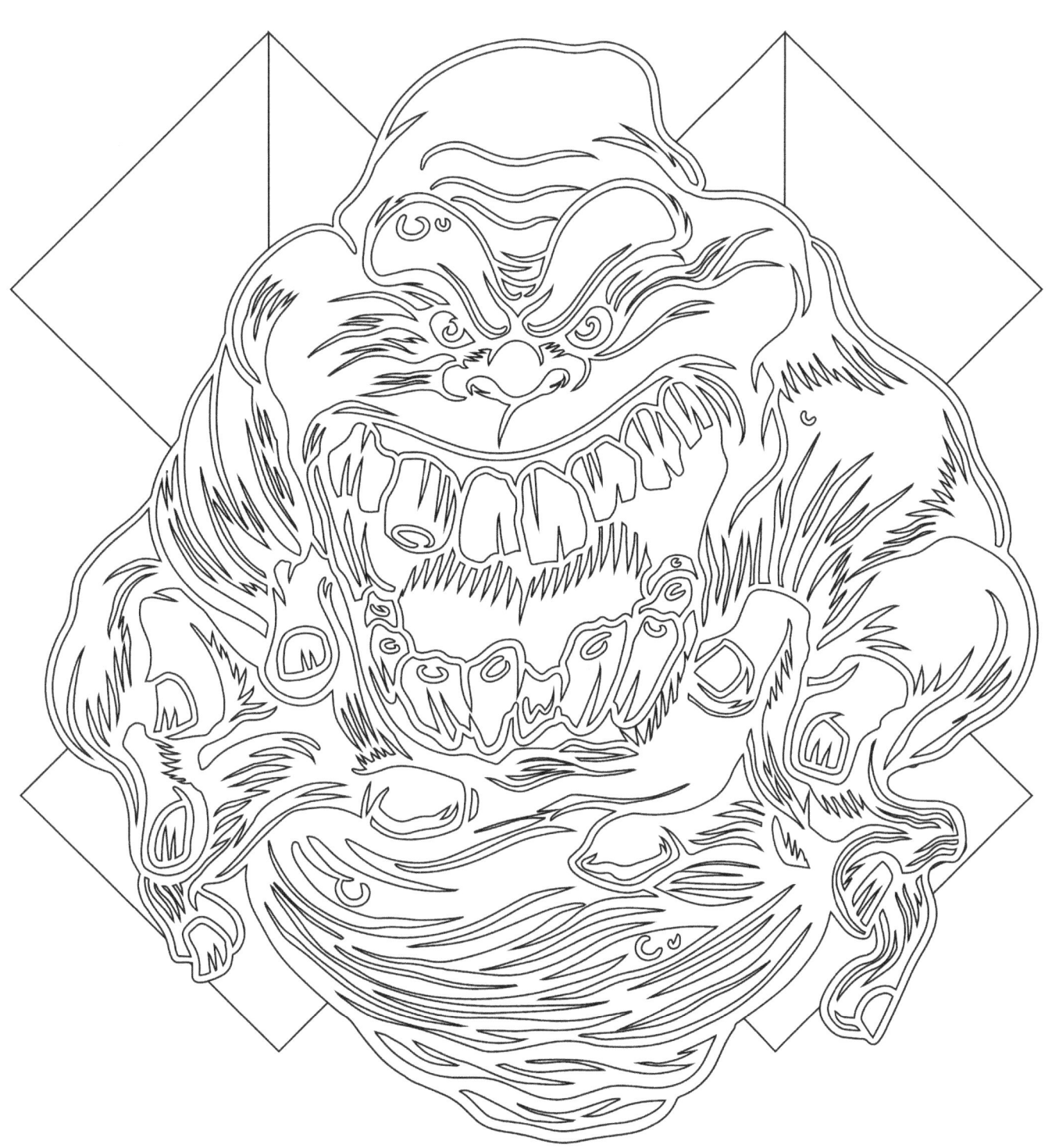

I'M NOT BUYING IT A
FUCKING BEER

GET READY TO COLOR.

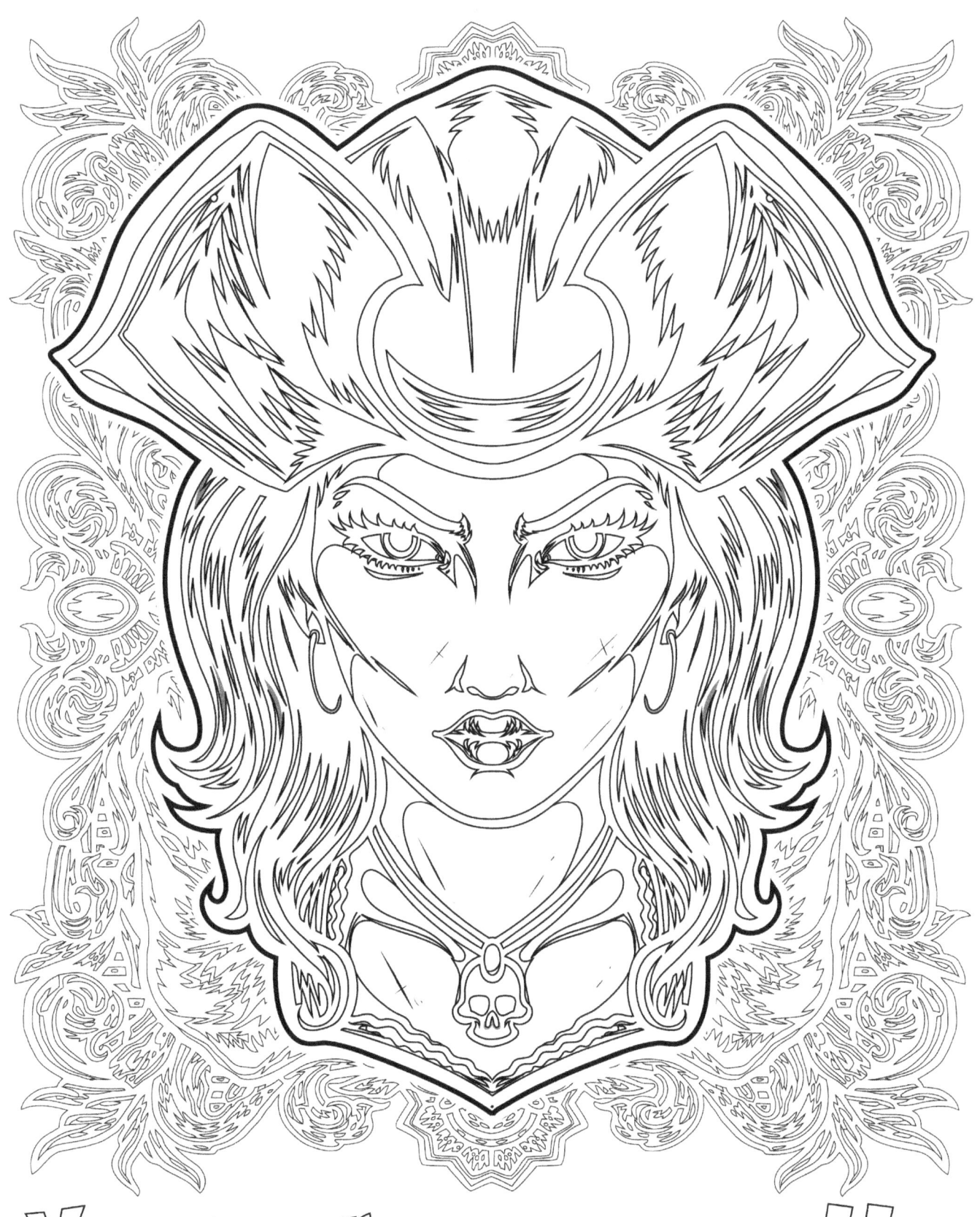

GET READY TO COLOR

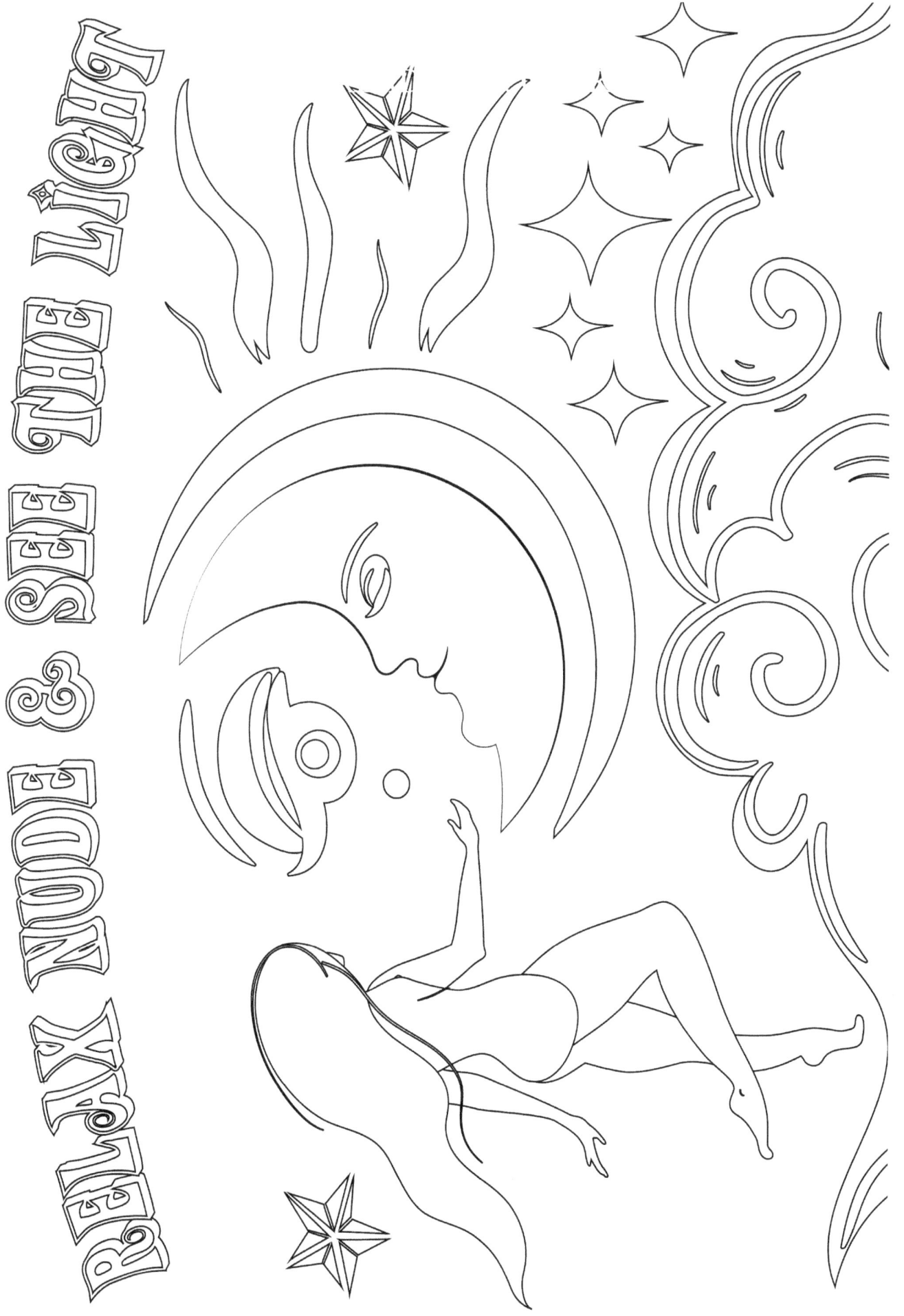

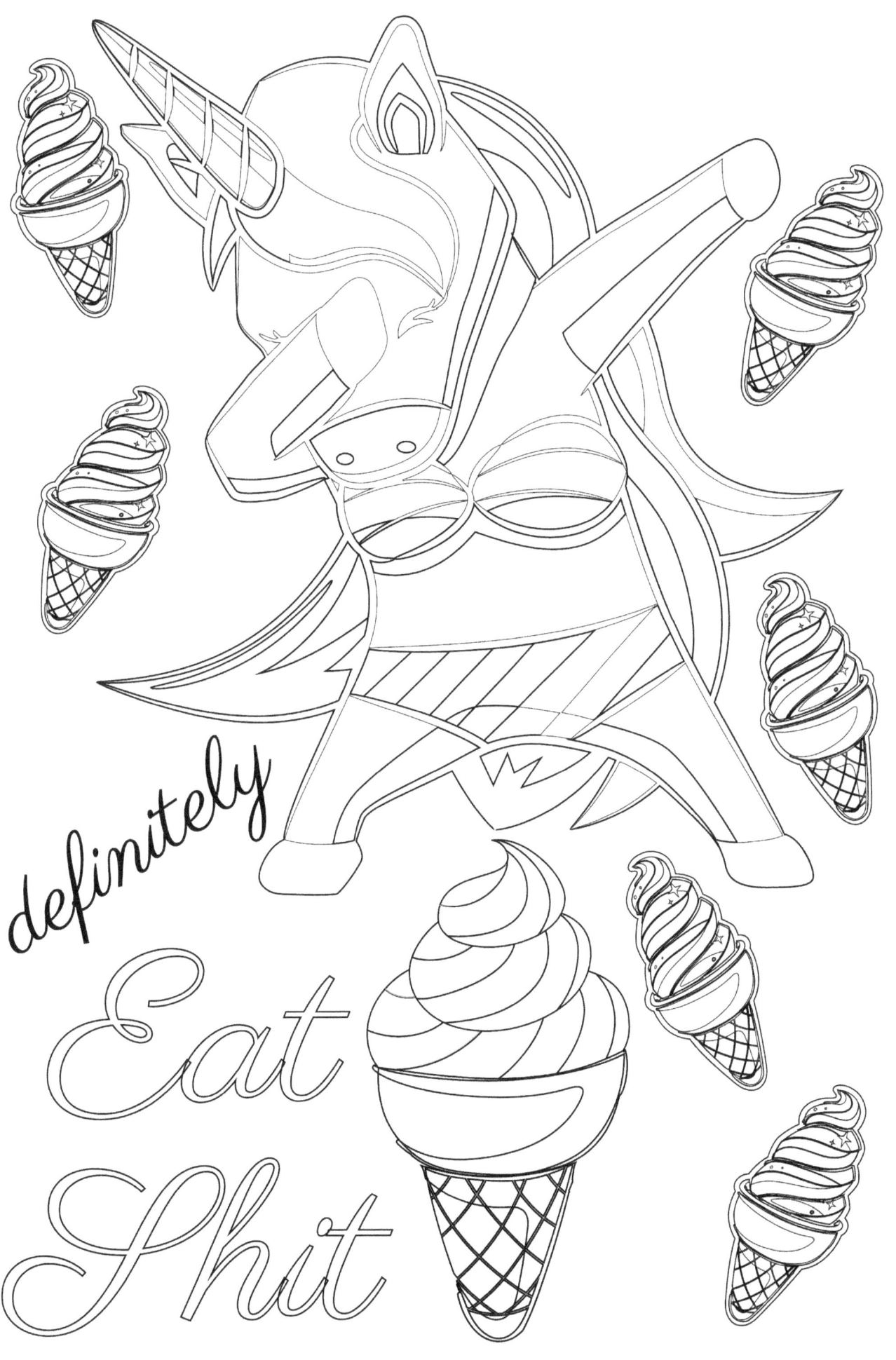

GET READY TO COLOR

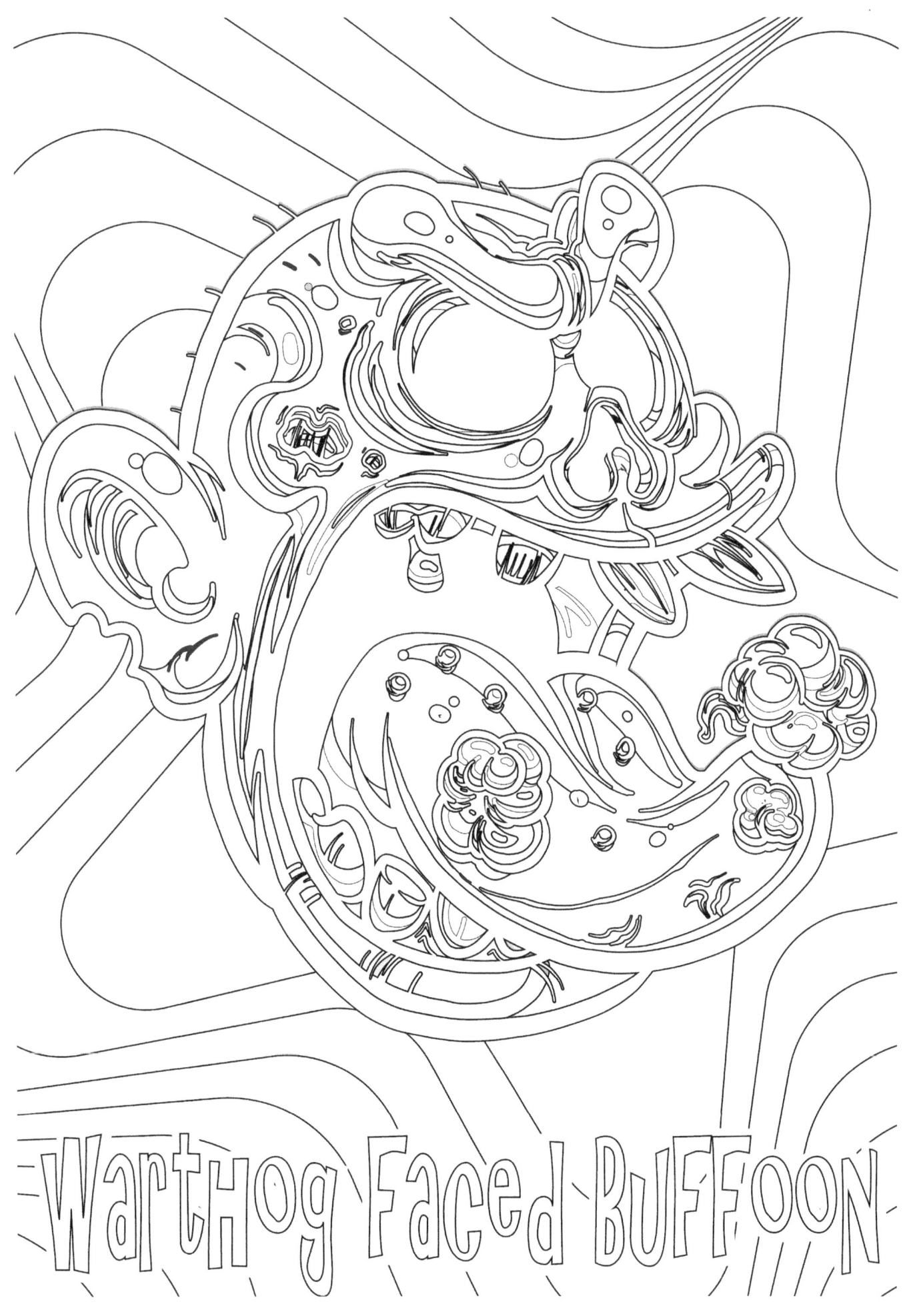

GET READY TO COLOR

I want to activate Your Star

GET READY TO COLOR

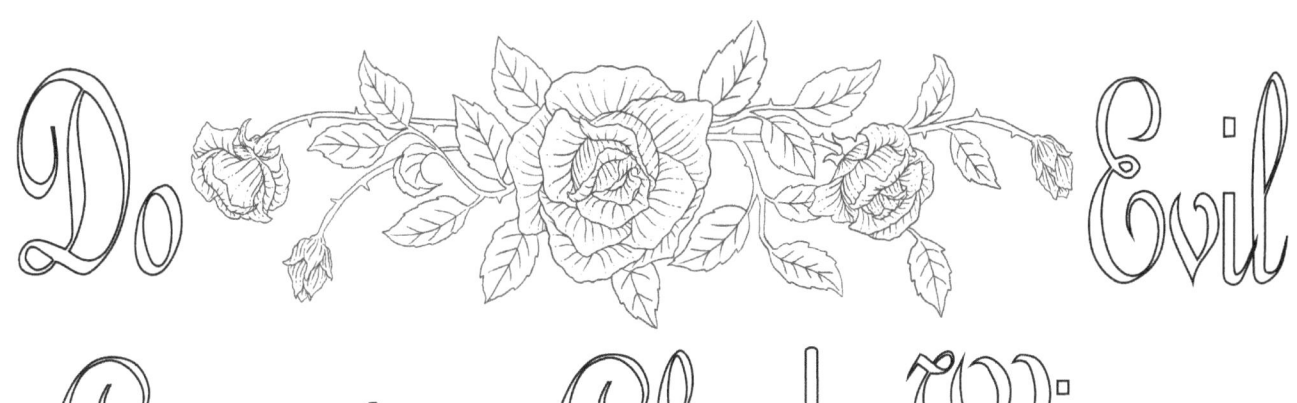

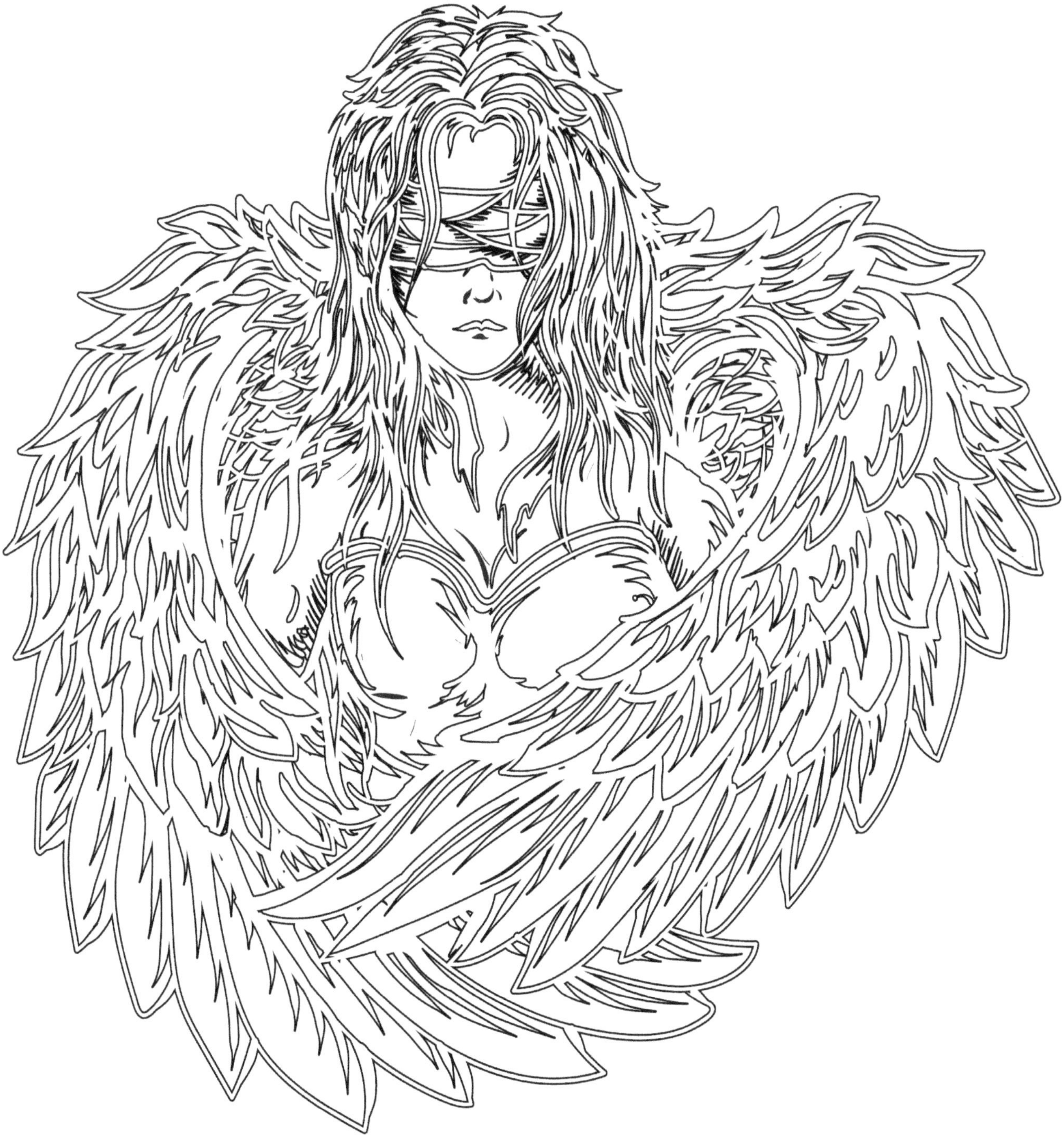

GET READY TO COLOR

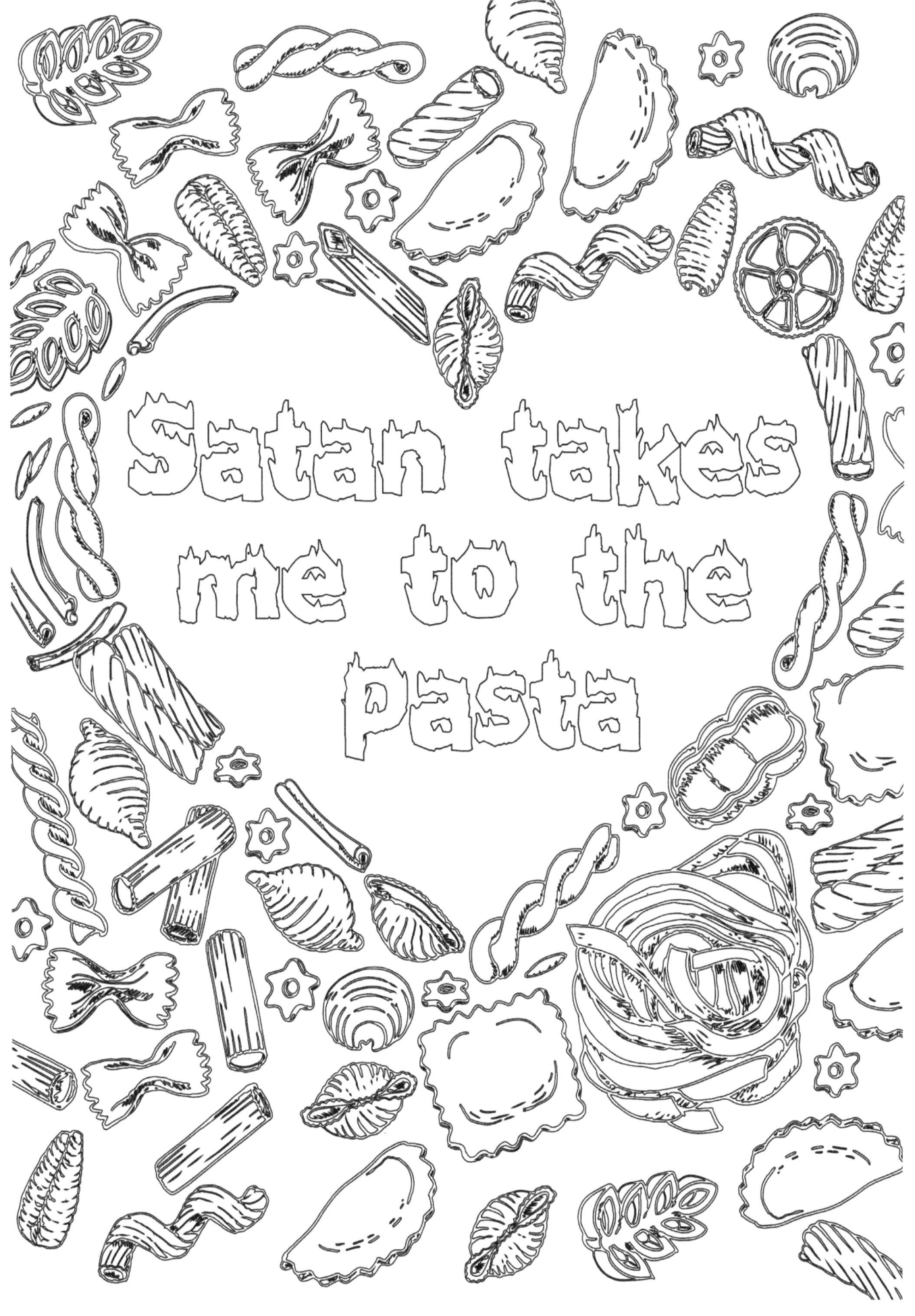

GET READY TO COLOR

My Heart Is Within The Egg

GET READY TO COLOR

What Ever Sprinkles

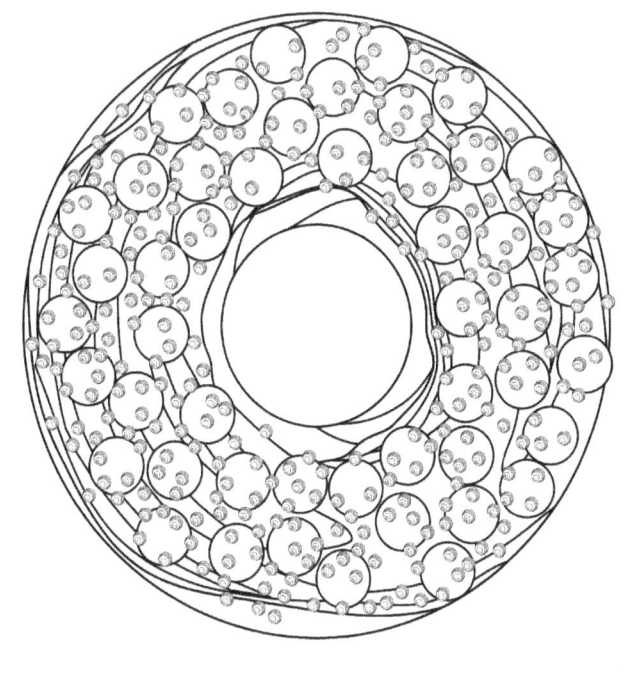 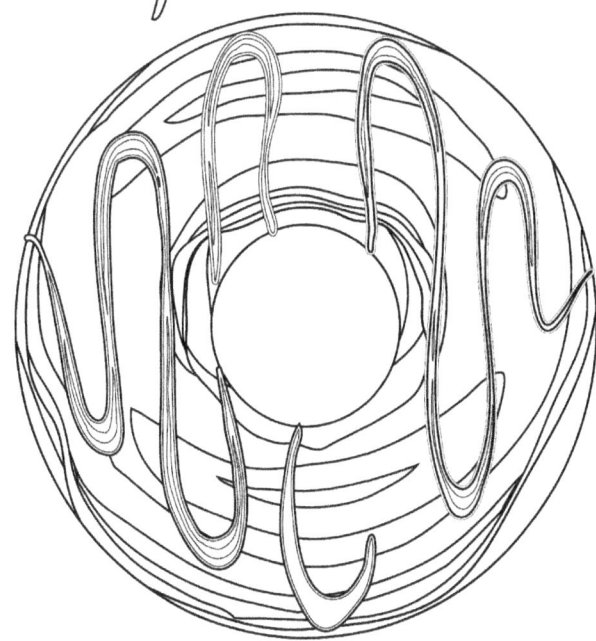

Your Donuts

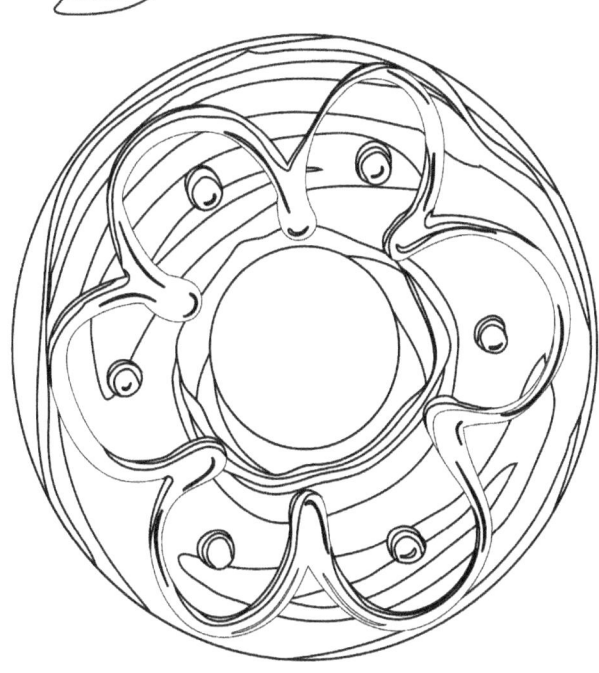 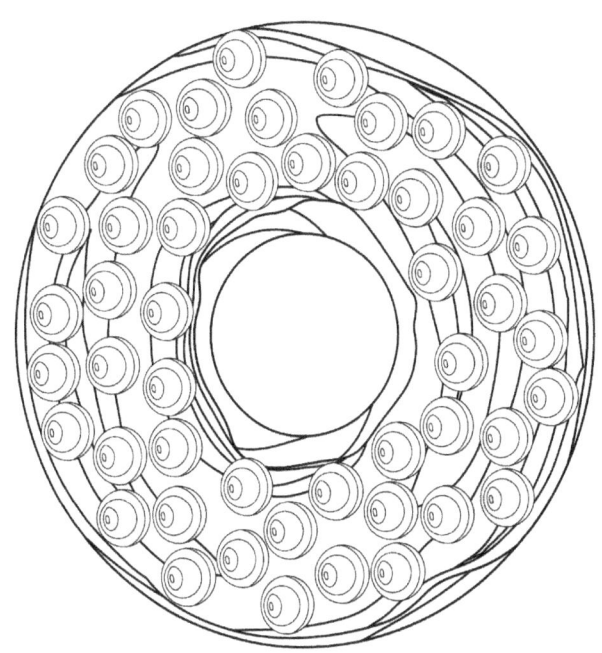

GET READY TO COLOR

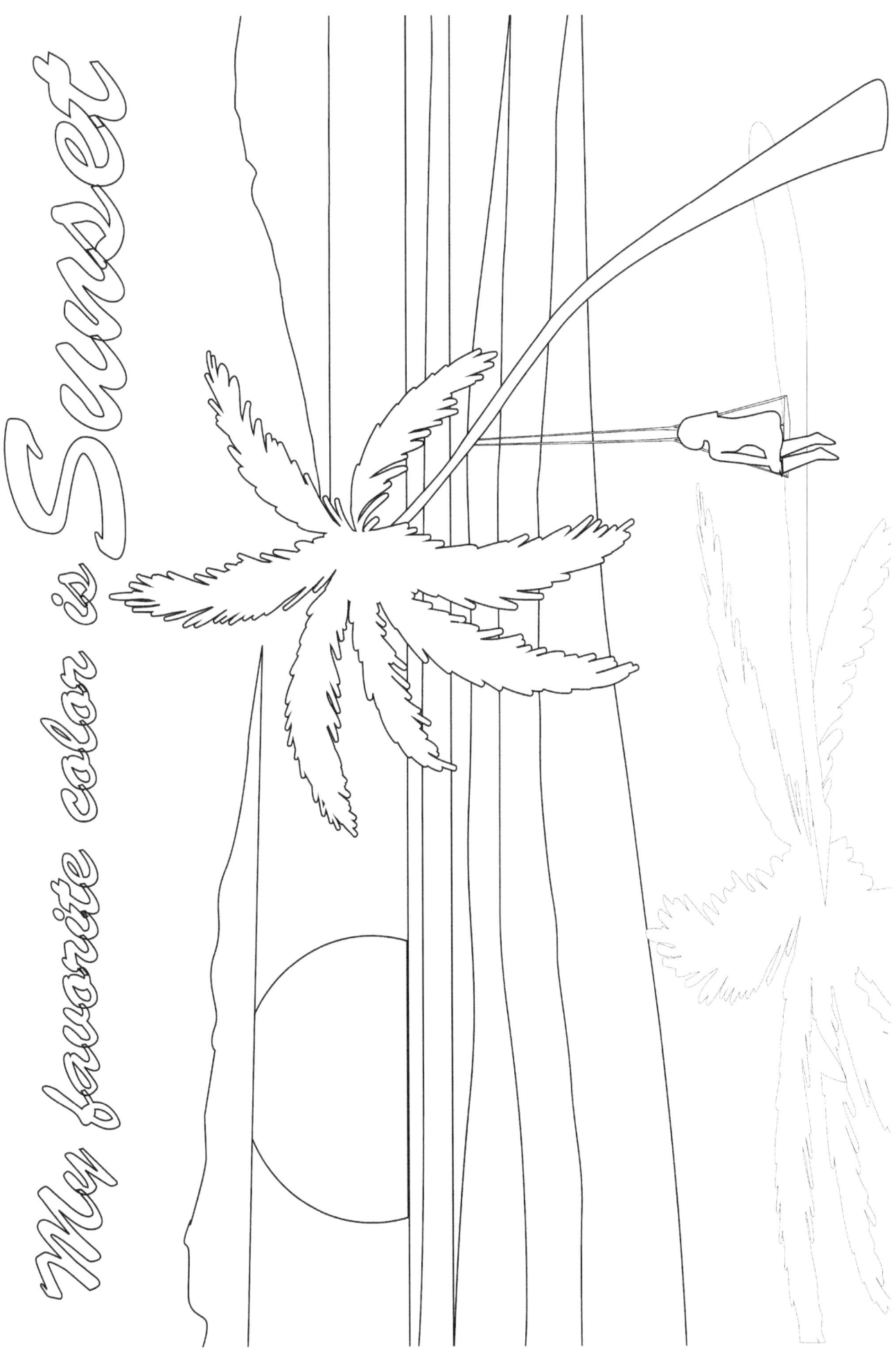

GET READY TO COLOR

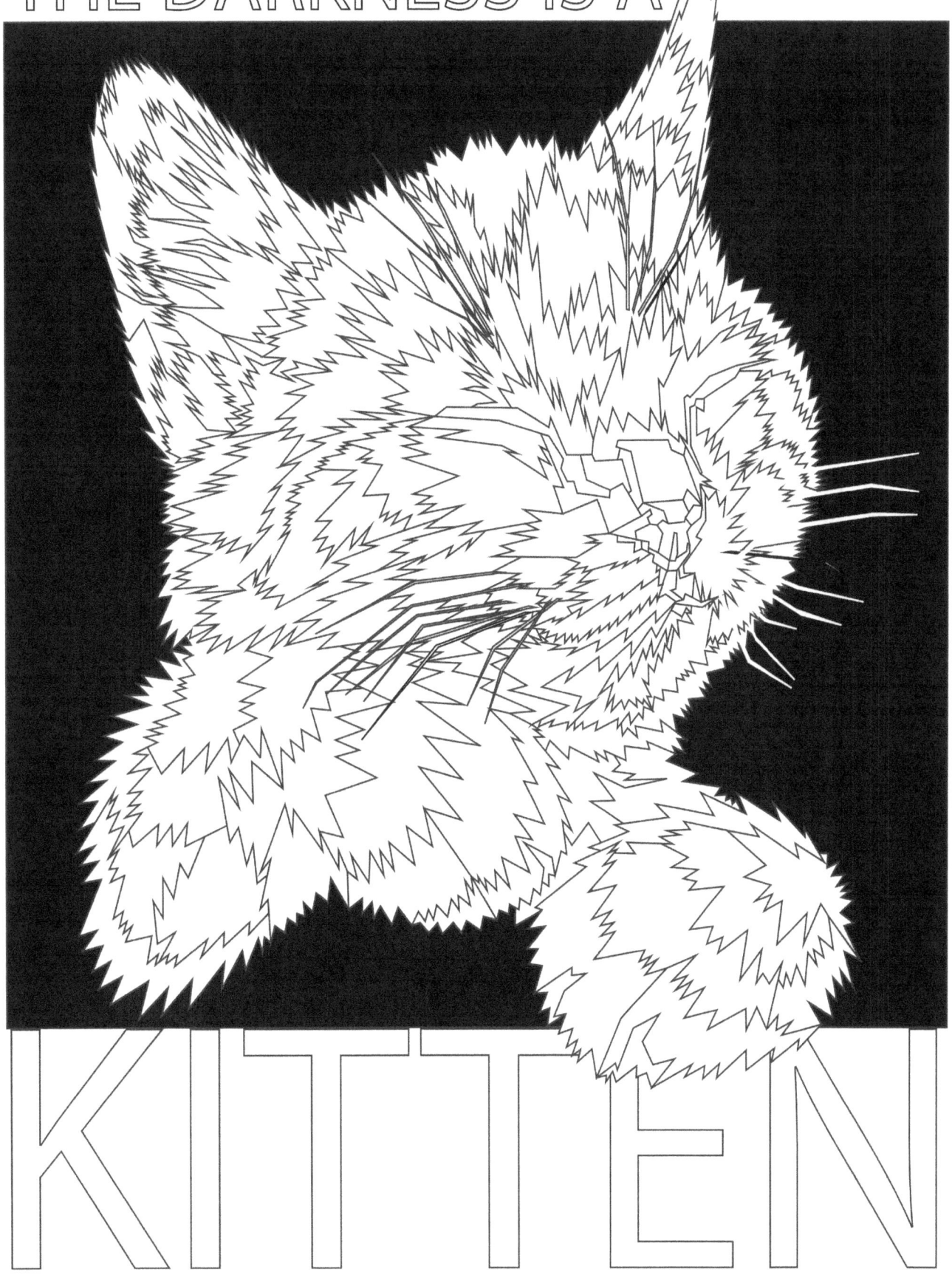

GET READY TO COLOR

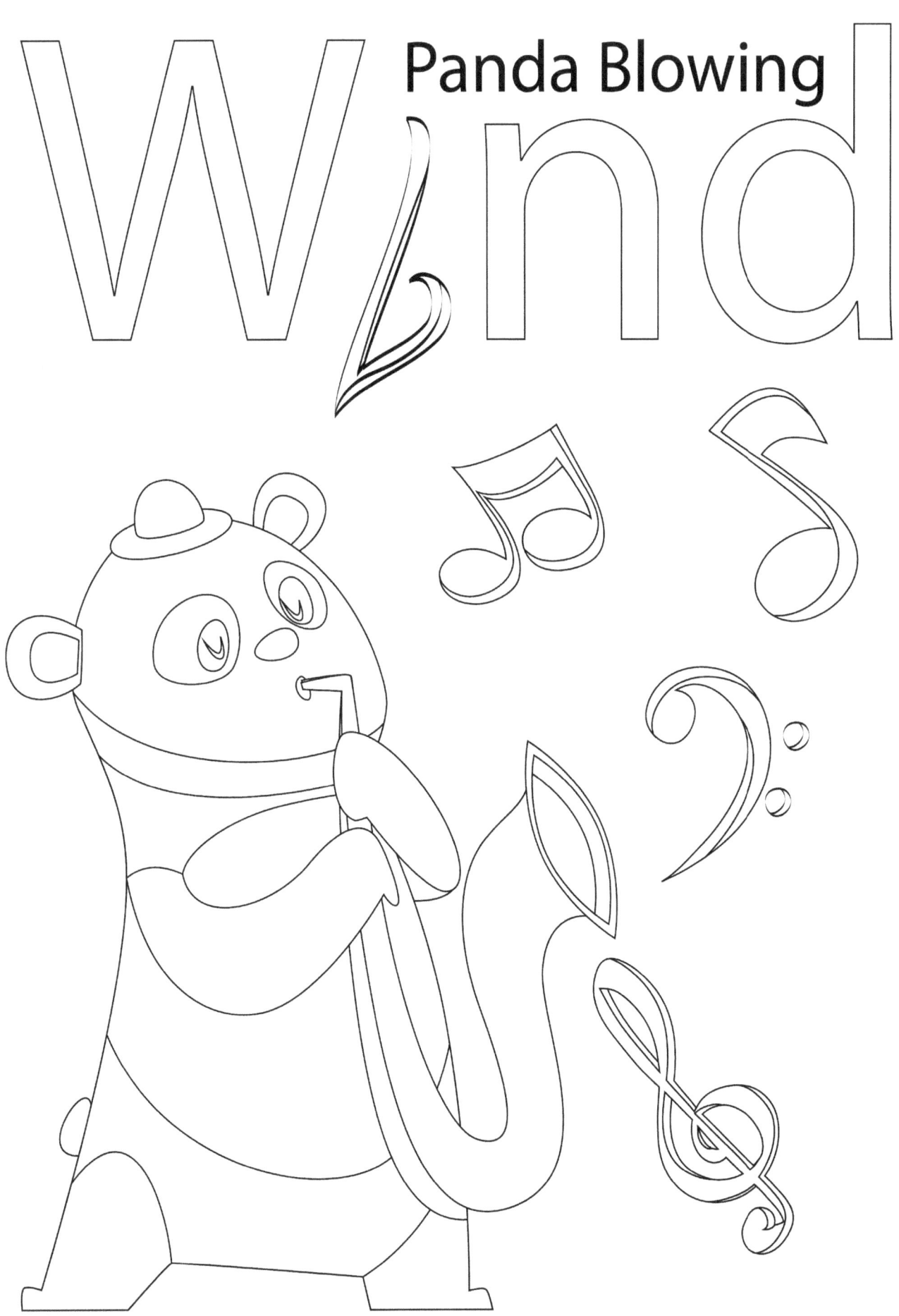

GET READY TO COLOR

GET READY TO COLOR

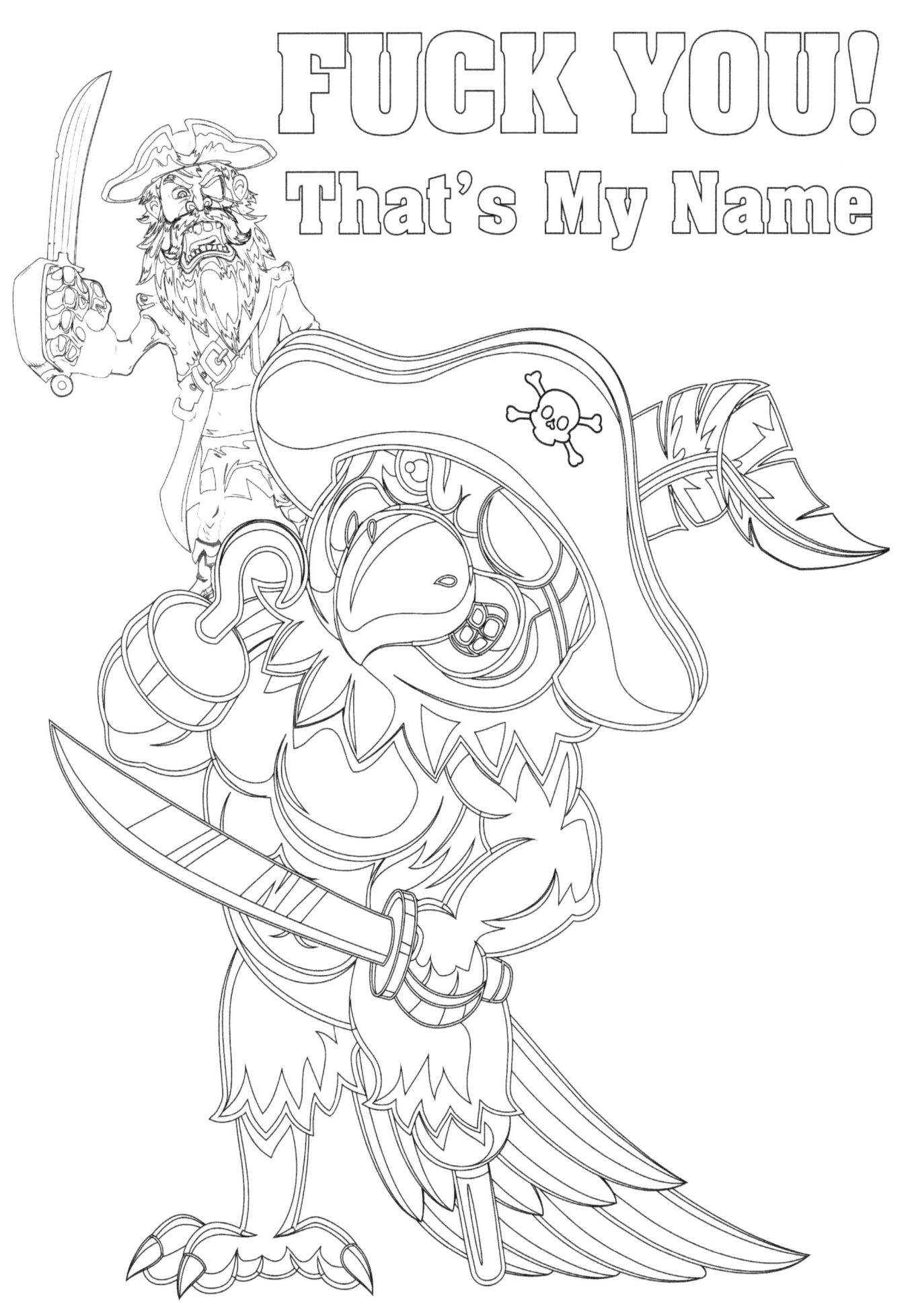

GET READY TO COLOR

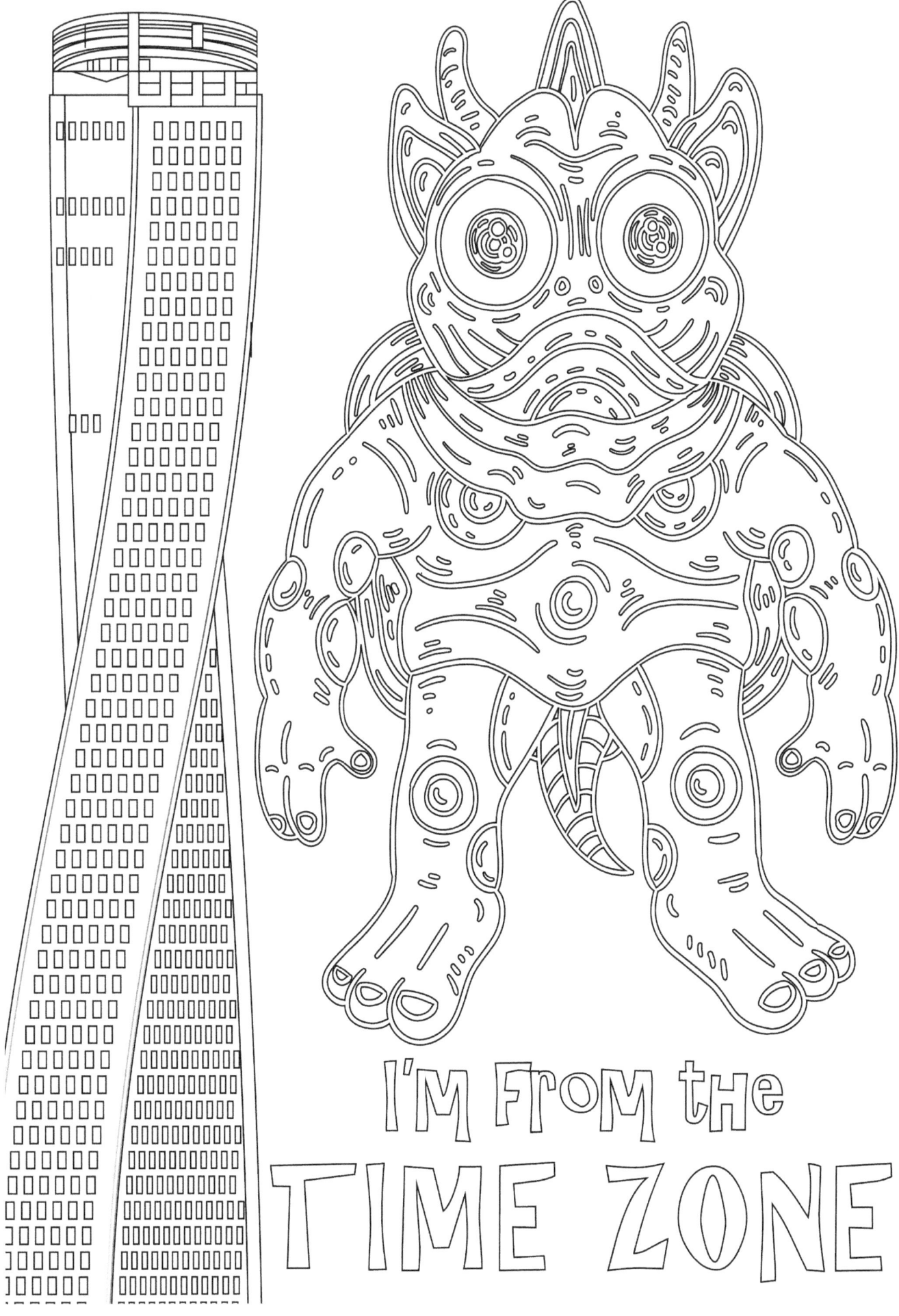

GET READY TO COLOR

keep yourself in Front of You

GET READY TO COLOR

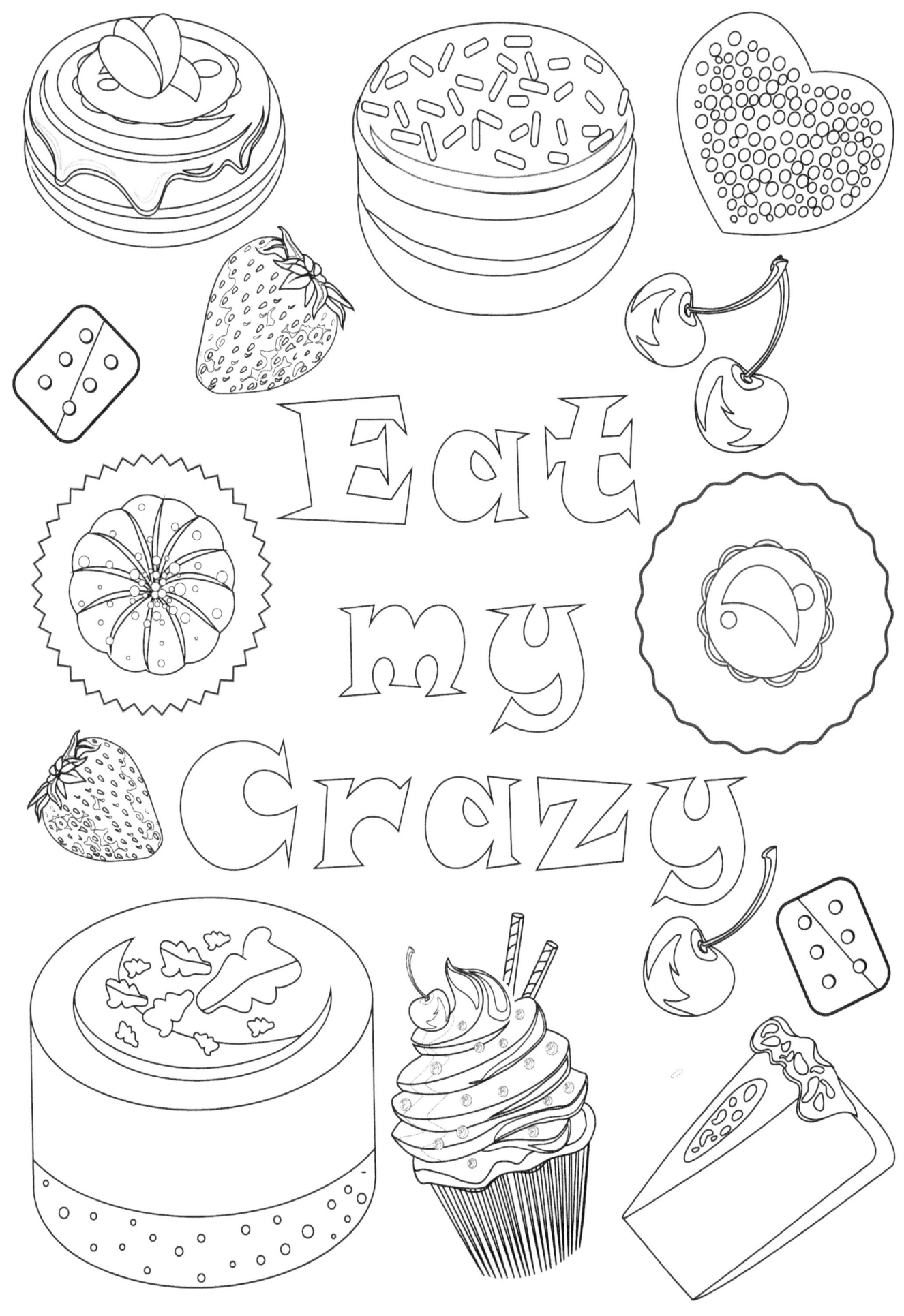

GET READY TO COLOR

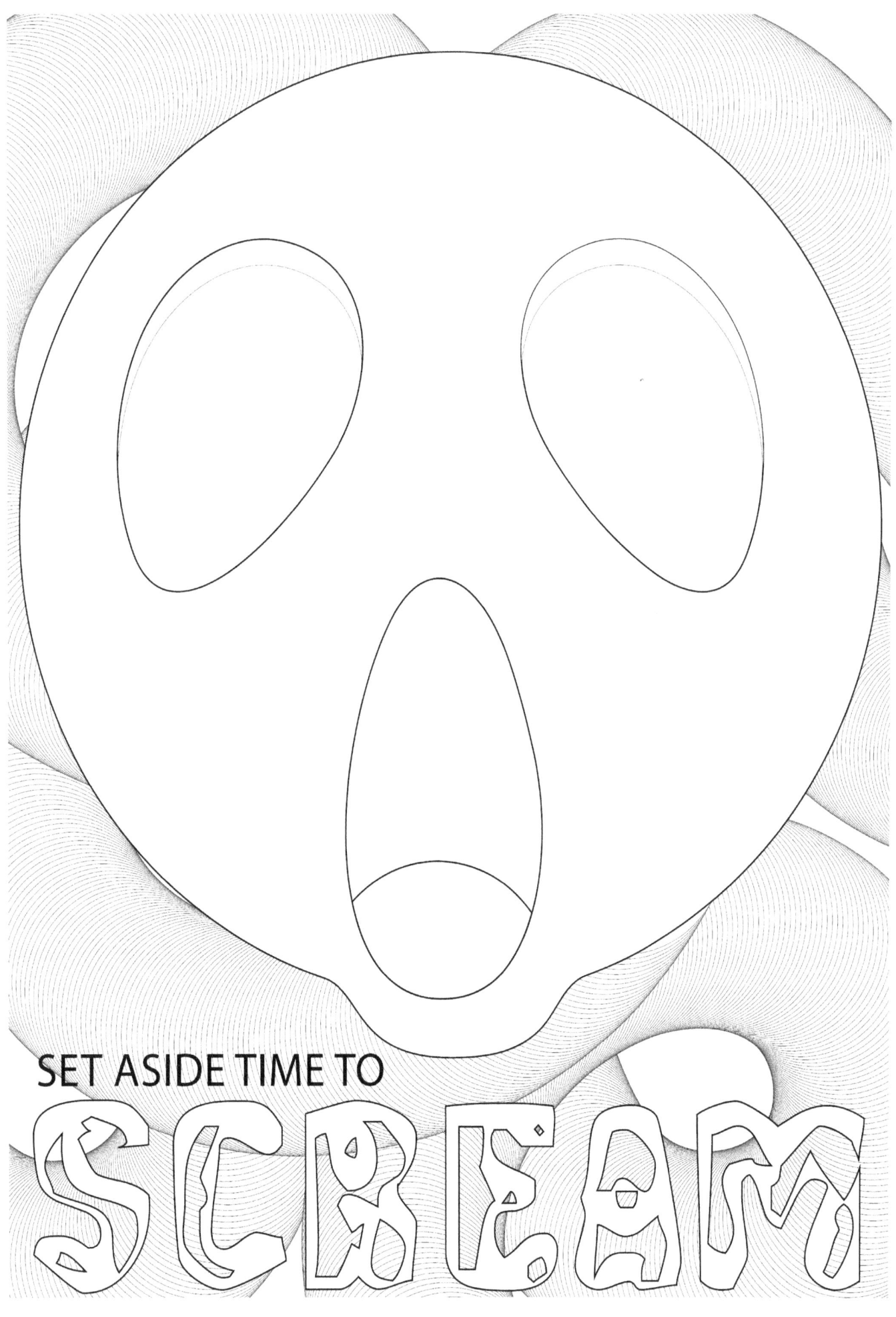

GET READY TO COLOR

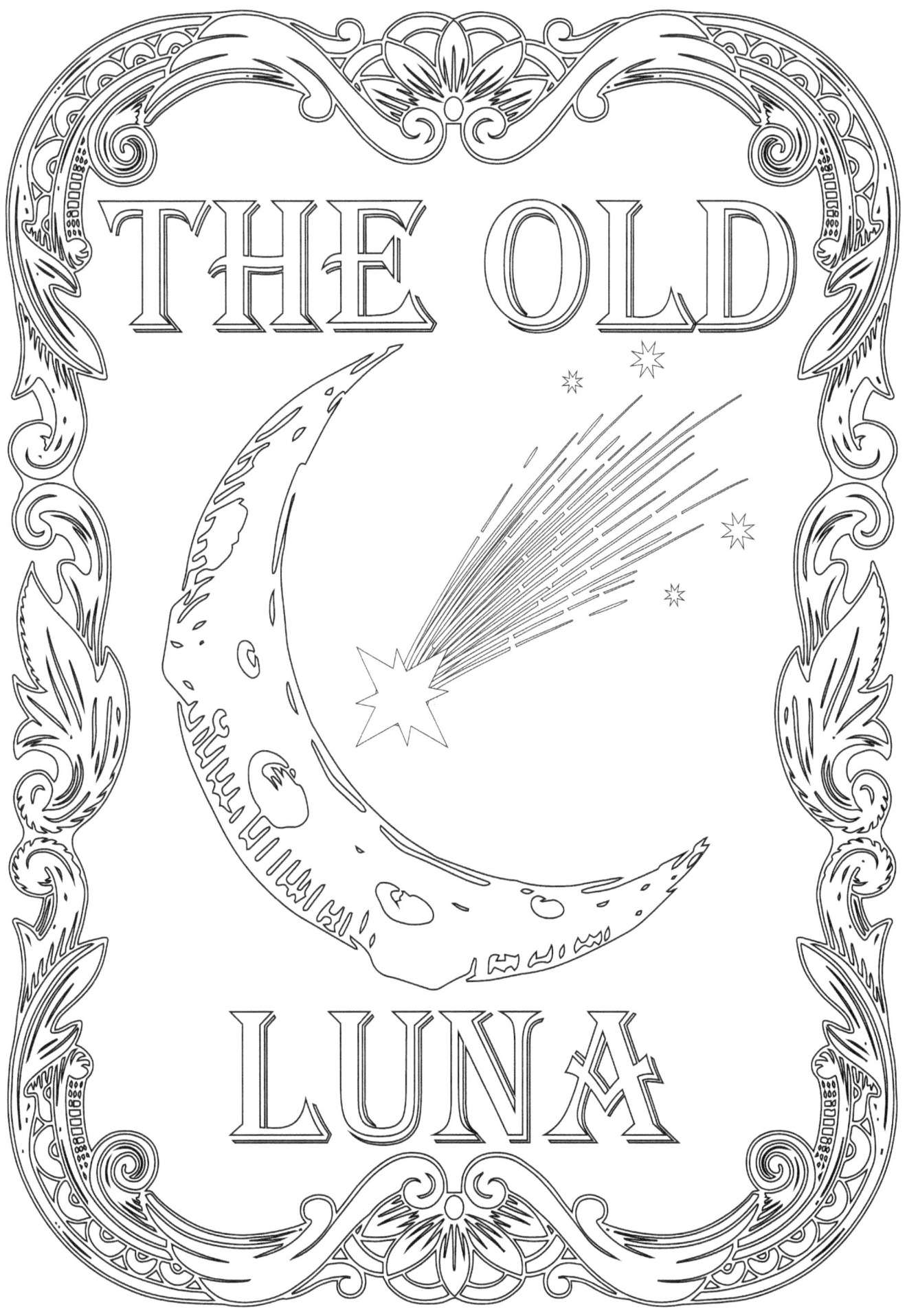

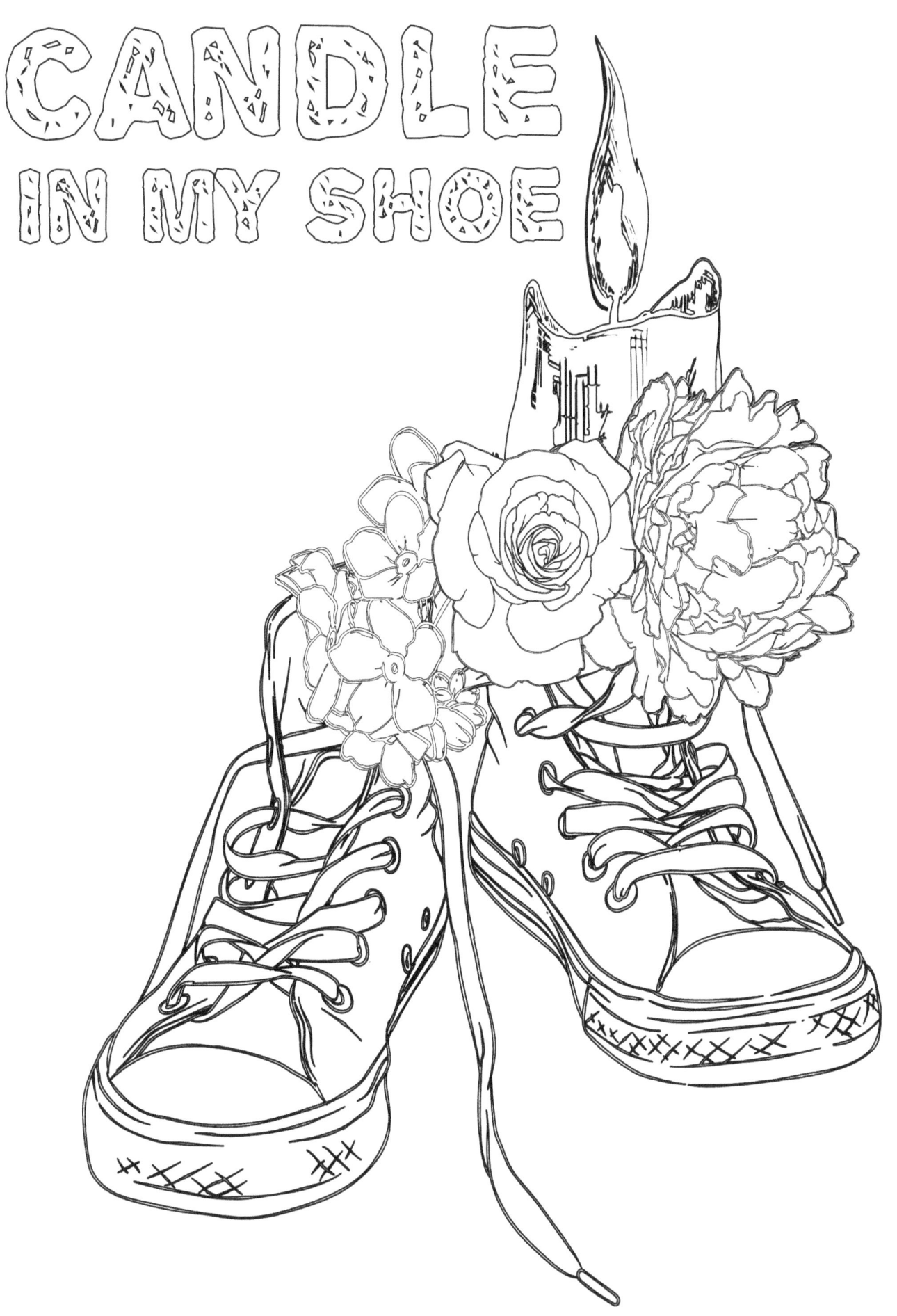

GET READY TO COLOR

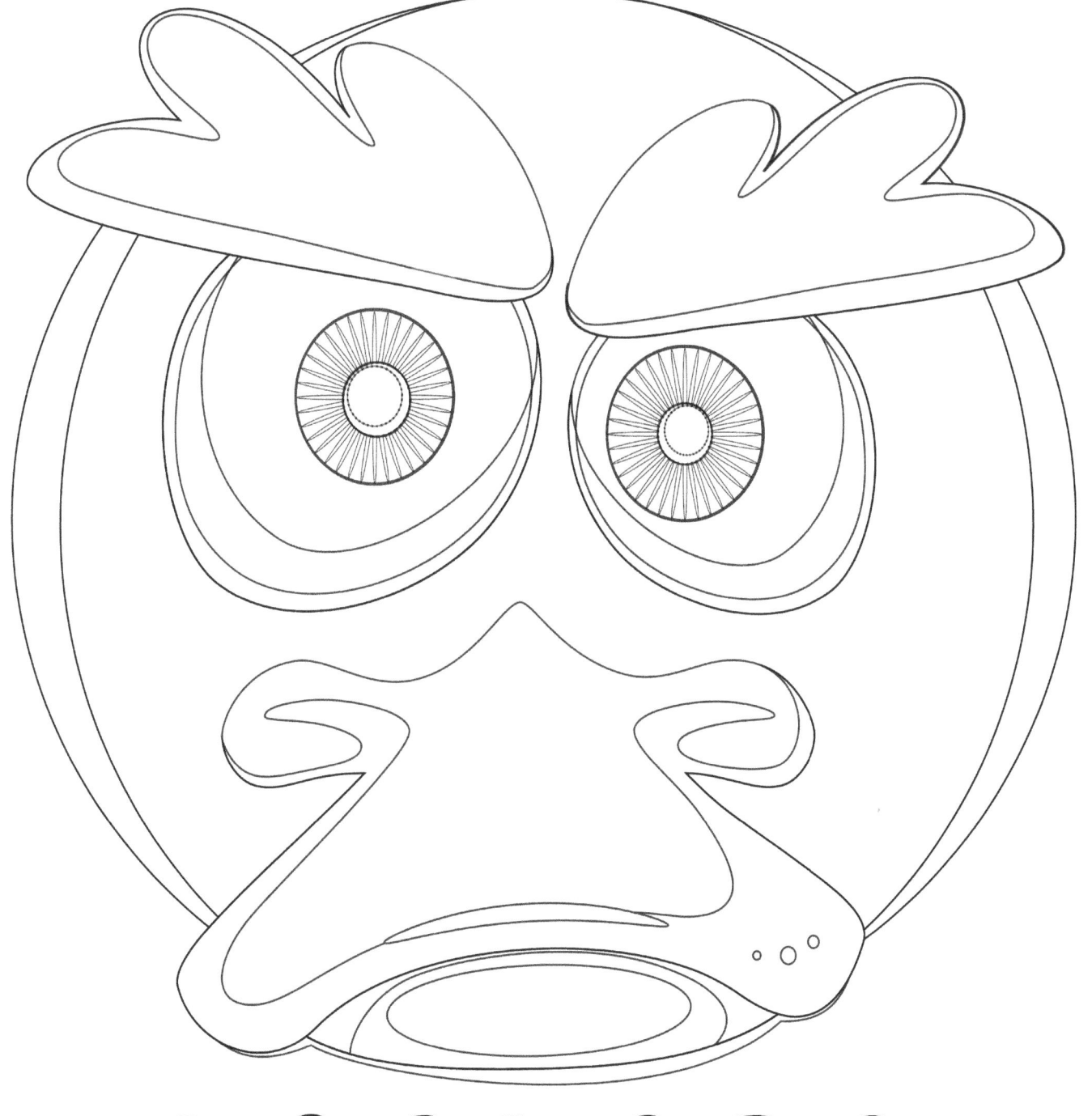

GET READY TO COLOR

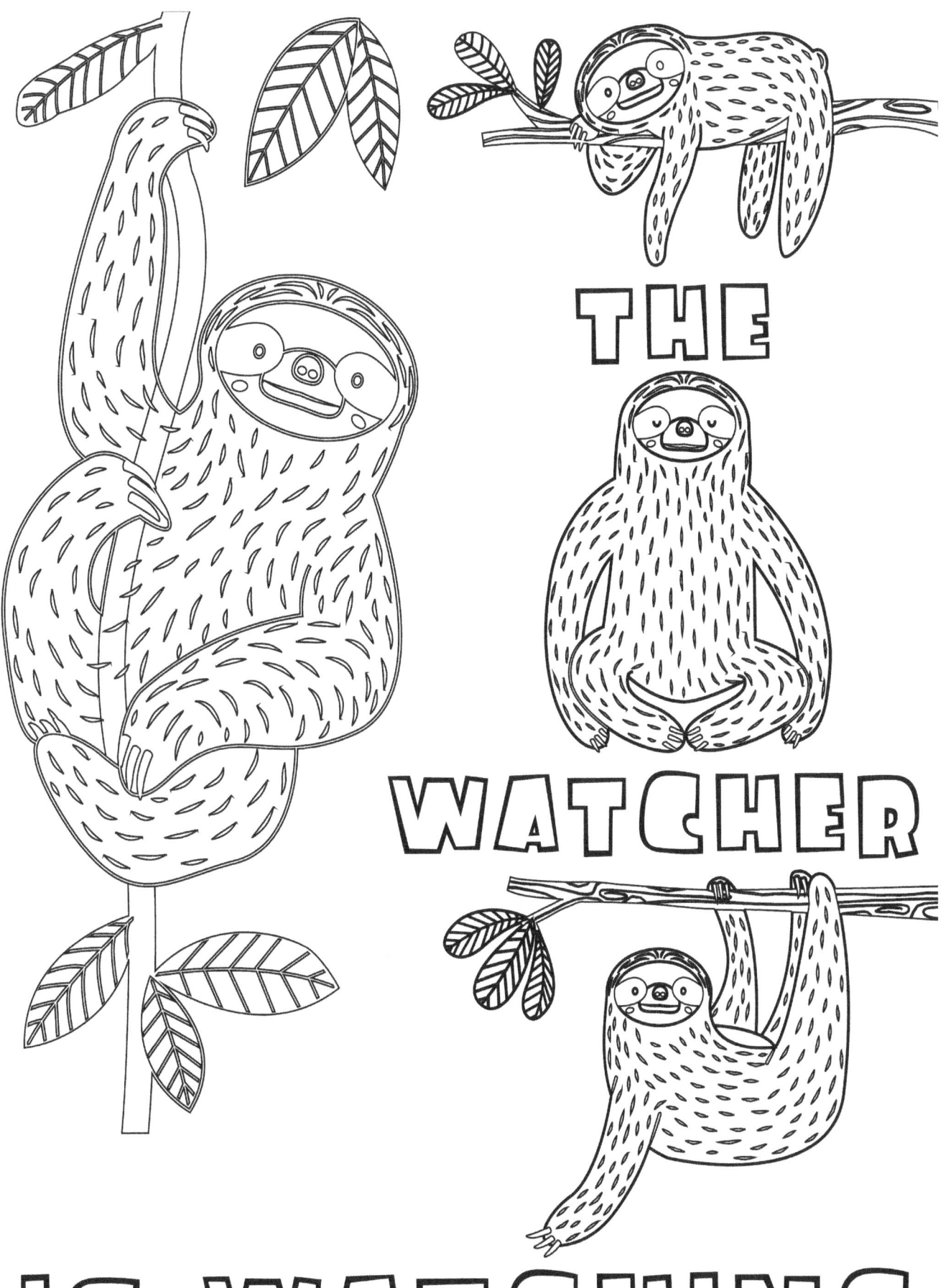

GET READY TO COLOR

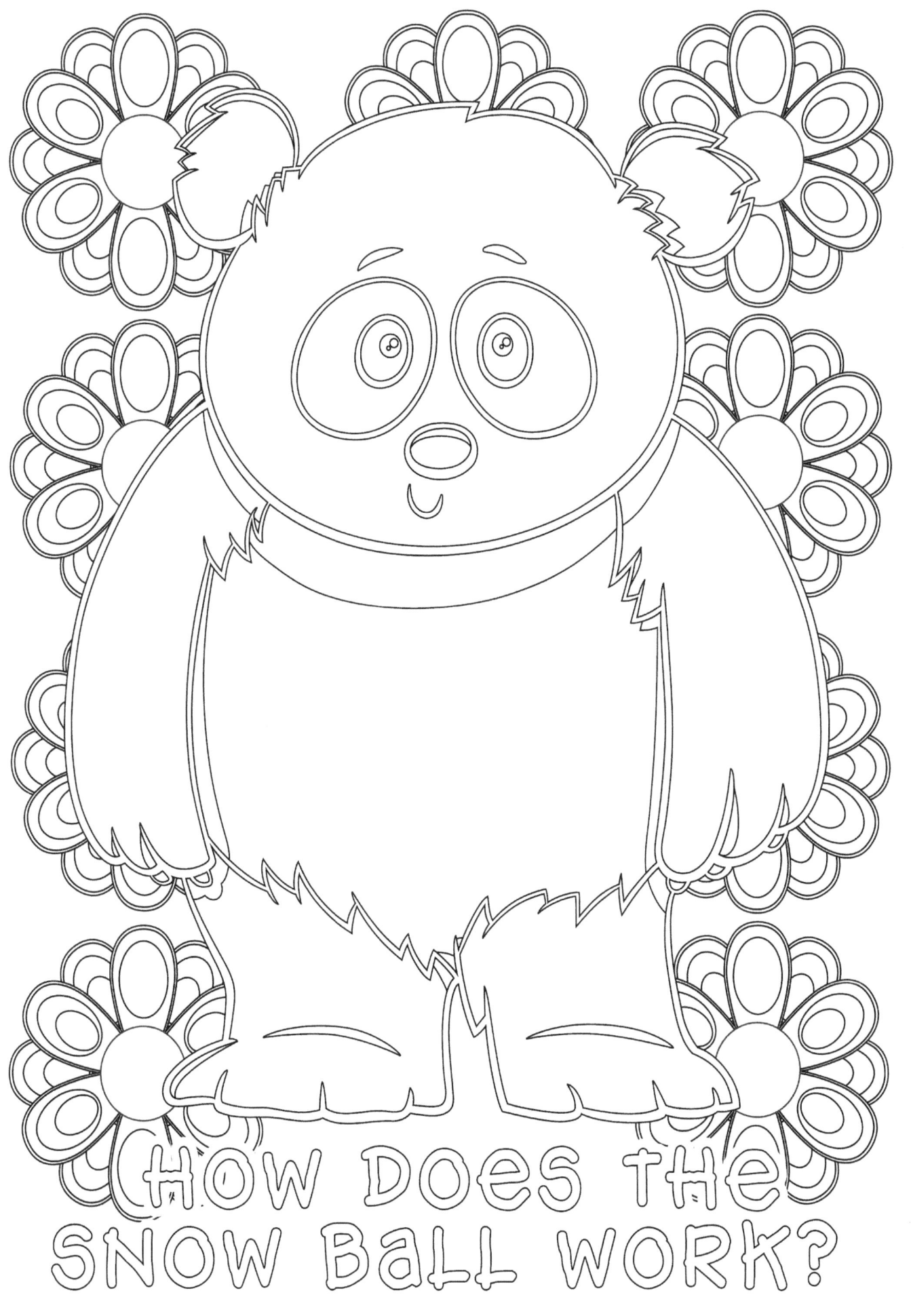

GET READY TO COLOR

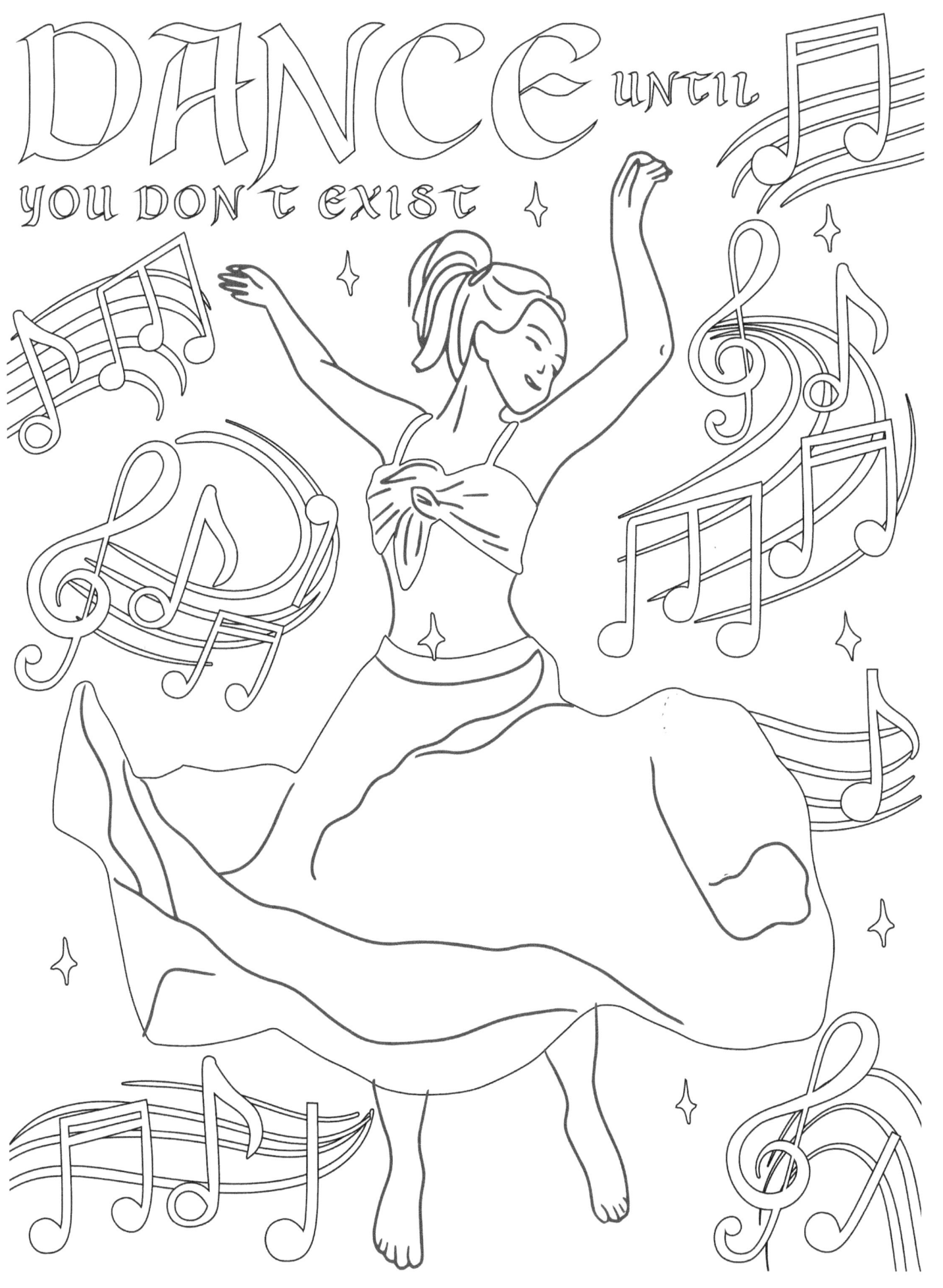

GET READY TO COLOR

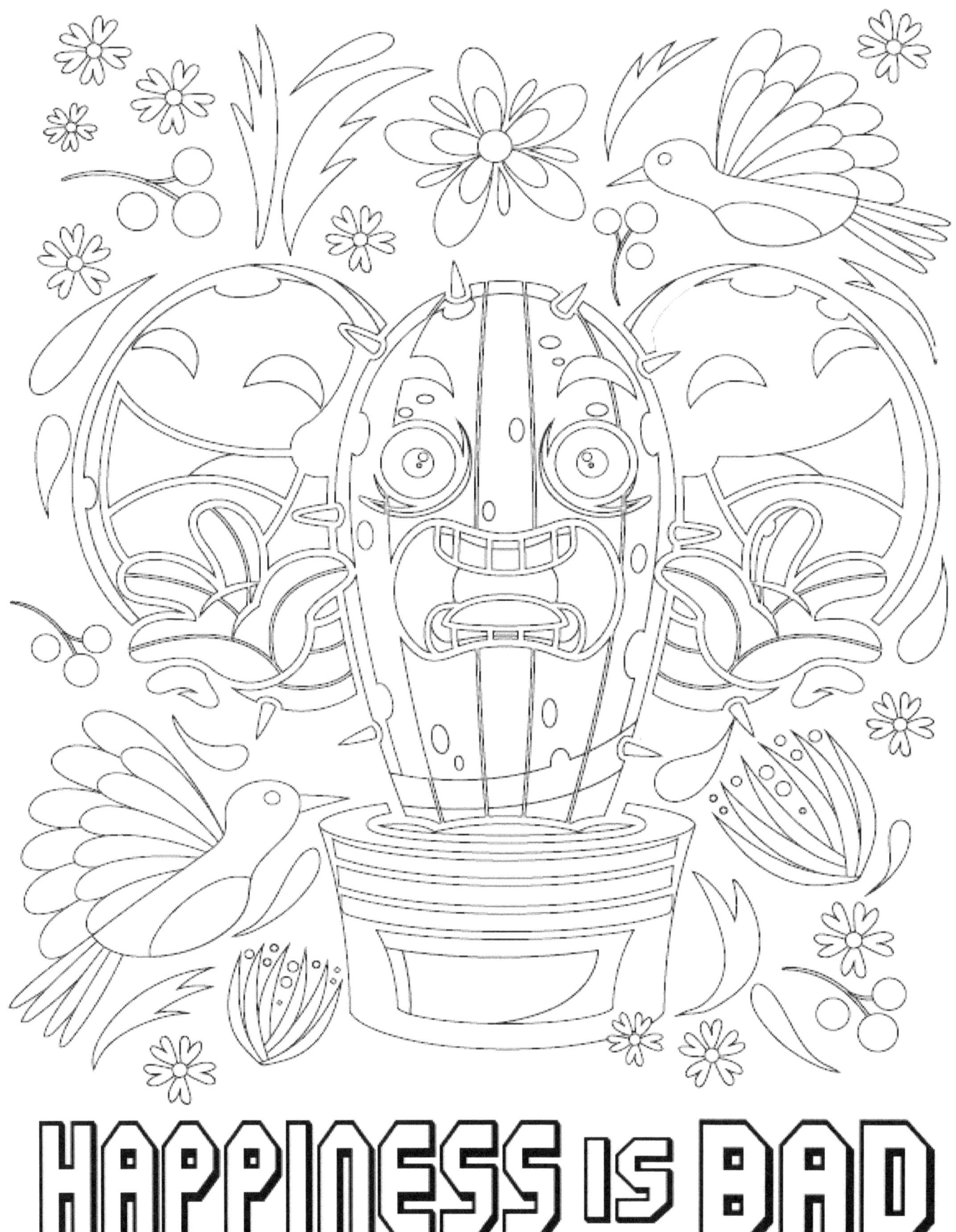

GET READY TO COLOR

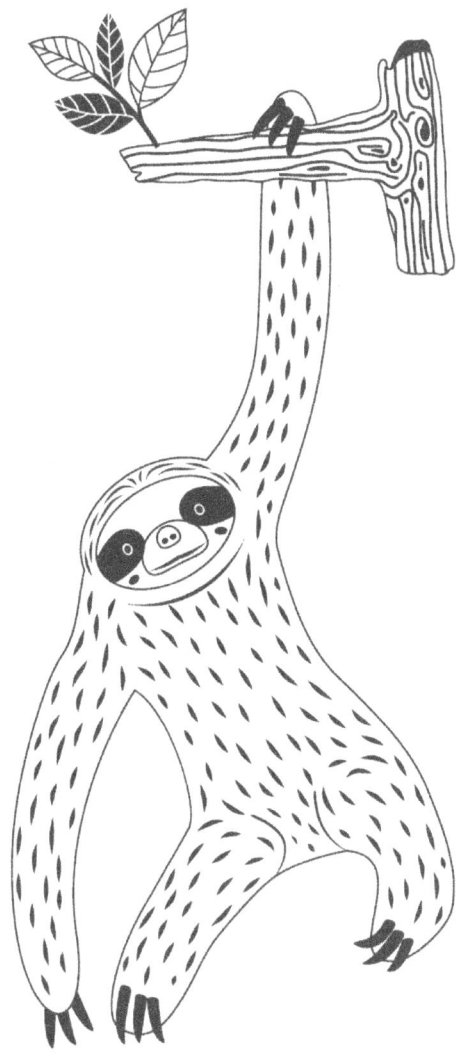

ACKNOWLEDGEMENTS

Appreciation goes out to those who contributed inspiration and support for my coloring books. Thanks to Rebecca Miller, Lea Johnson and Dale Franks. Everyone who has supported this edition extends their hope that readers have found it to be fun and entertaining.

AFTERWORD

If you have any thoughts, suggestions or tips for my next coloring book, please contact the author. Your feedback is welcome.

Reviews are gold to authors! If you've enjoyed this book Please consider rating or reviewing it. Comments and suggestions are appreciated and help me improve future titles.

www.ingramcontent.com/pod-product-compliance
Lightning Source LLC
Chambersburg PA
CBHW080529220526
45465CB00006B/2651